GRANNY'S KITCHEN

CORNISH COOKING FROM BACKALONG

Collected by Betty Waller.

Cover photograph

"Crust time" at the Dalcoath mines, Cornwall. 1906
(Frith)

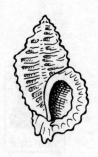

First published 1994 by
Whistlestop
Calstock,
Cornwall.
PL18 9SG.

Overall layout and design are by Colonel Mustard Design and
Illustration. Plymouth. Tel: 0752 794492.

British Library Cataloguing-in-Publication Data.
A catalogue record of this book is available from the British Library.

ISBN 0-9519778-1-4

Printed and Bound by Caradon Printers, Higher Metherell,
Callington, Cornwall

CONTENTS

INTRODUCTION

My thanks are due to all the Cornish Grannies who have racked their brains to recall the recipes their mothers used.

The Cornish tin miners and fishermen were no strangers to poverty and hard times, and the ability of a housewife to feed her hungry family - often with the most unpromising of ingredients, was all important.

Indeed it was an old joke that the devil never came into Cornwall for fear of being made into a pie!

There was a rhyme which said it all:

> Gurty milk an' bearly-bread no lack,
> Pudden-skins an ' a good-shaip's chack,
> A bussa o' salt pelchers, 'nother o' pork,
> A good strong stummick and plenty o' work.

One or two of these recipes might have needed 'a good strong stomach', certainly none of them need microwaves. They will be a challenge - but then half the fun is in the trying.

Betty Waller,

Calstock,
Cornwall.
1994.

SOUPS

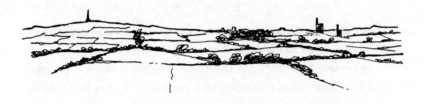

KETTLE or KIDDLY BROTH

6 onions	2 rounds of bread
knob of butter	seasoning

Boil the six onions, strain and pour the liquid into a basin on top of bread which has been cut into squares; add a knob of butter, pepper and salt to taste. Eat very hot.

MACARONI SOUP

3oz of macaroni	walnut sized knob of butter
2 quarts of clear stock	seasoning

Throw the macaroni and butter into boiling water with a pinch of salt, and allow to simmer for half-an-hour. When tender, dry and cut into thin rings or lengths, and drop into the boiling stock and stew gently for five minutes. Serve with grated cheese.

FISH SOUP

1 average sized haddock	1 large onion chopped small
whiting or pollack	knob of butter
pepper and salt	1½ oz of flour
1 pint of milk	

Place fish in saucepan. Add 2 pints of water and boil it until the fish shreds easily. Strain off the liquid into a saucepan, adding a pint of milk, 1 large onion chopped small, a knob of butter, pepper and salt. Simmer it until thoroughly cooked and serve up hot. If need be thicken with 1½ ozs of flour, and garnish with a little finely chopped parsley.

NETTLE BROTH

2 pints of stock	2 pints of young
flour	nettles
2 blades of chives	5 tblsp of oat or
seasoning	barley

Clean the nettles, plunge into boiling salt water and boil for 15 minutes. Put into a colander and wash in fresh running water. Cut up fine with chives, sprinkle with flour and then frizzle in a little fat. Add stock and boil gently in a closed pan for hour. Skim well, season and serve.

MUTTON BROTH

1½ lbs of knuckle	2 small carrots
of mutton	1 stalk of celery
3 leeks	1 small turnip
seasoning	1 tsp of barley
3 pints cold water	[soak overnight]
1 tsp parsley chopped fine	

Wipe the meat with a damp cloth. Cut it away from the bone in small pieces, remove all fat, slice the vegetables thinly.

Place meat, bones and water in a saucepan, add salt to taste. Cover and bring slowly to the boil. Skim well and add the barley. Simmer the soup for 2 to 3 hours, or until the meat and vegetables are well cooked. Before serving remove the bones, and skim off any grease from the top of the broth. Add more salt if necessary.

BEETROOT SOUP

4 boiled beetroots	1 good sized onion
bones or beef	juice of 2 lemons

Skin and slice thinly 4 boiled beetroots, and 1 good sized onion. Add some bones or beef and seasoning. Cover with cold water and boil for one hour. Add the juice of two lemons, strain and serve hot.

GIBLET SOUP

2 sets of giblets	1 quart of water
seasoning	sweet herbs
carrot	onion
flour	milk
mace	

Wash, scald and cut up 2 sets of giblets, break the bones of the necks, and divide the heads into two. Boil them up gradually in 1 quart of water. Skim once or twice, add seasoning, mace, sweet herbs, carrot and onion, and simmer for 2 hours. Remove giblets and thicken with flour and milk. Serve soup and meat together.

CELERY SOUP

9 heads of celery	1 tsp salt
nutmeg to taste	1 lump of sugar
½ pint of strong stock	1 pint of cream
2 quarts of boiling water	

Cut the celery into small pieces, throw into the water, seasoned with the nutmeg, salt and sugar. Boil until tender, pass through a sieve, add the stock and simmer for half-an-hour. Put in the cream, bring it to boiling point and serve.

KIDNEY SOUP

1 ox kidney	1 marrow bone
1 carrot	parsley
seasoning	4 pints of water

Remove the fat and cut the ox kidney into squares. Soak it in boiling water for one hour, wash well, cover with water, boil quickly and then stew slowly for two hours. Put a marrow bone, carrot and a little parsley into another saucepan, add 4 pints of water and boil for 1½ hours. Remove all the bones and vegetables. Season and add to kidney. Boil for another hour and skim before serving.

CARROT and LENTIL SOUP

3 quarts of stock	1 pint of lentils
4 carrots sliced	2 onions sliced
1 lettuce shredded	2 tblsp cooked rice
2 oz butter	seasoning

Soak the lentils all night, then drain. Heat the butter in a saucepan, put in the vegetables, and let them fry slowly for 15 minutes. Add lentils and stock, season with salt and pepper, and simmer gently for 1 hour. Pass through a sieve, return to the saucepan, add the cooked rice, and serve very hot.

FISH DISHES

To Choose Fish

The flesh should be firm, the eyes bright, and the gills red.
A proof of freshness in most fish is in their being covered in scales.
Avoid very large fish, for if old their fibres may be very tough.
A flat fish should be thick in proportion to its size.
Fish should have large girth rather than great length.
Large herrings, large whitings, but small fresh haddock, soles and plaice of medium size should be selected.
Lobsters and crabs should be heavy in proportion to their size.

BAKED COD WITH OATMEAL STUFFING

1 middle cut of cod	2 cupsful of oatmeal
2 onions	seasoning
butter and dripping	½ cupful of milk

Wash thoroughly, and remove the fins, and then put on a baking dish and securely skewer. Stuff with the following stuffing:- take 2 cupsful of oatmeal, and make moist with a mixture of butter and good dripping; add the 2 onions, finely chopped, and pepper and salt to taste. Pour a little milk around the fish, and bake slowly for an hour. Serve with white sauce and mashed potatoes.

MARINATED MACKEREL

4 or more mackerel	2 chopped bay leaves
6 cloves	blade of mace
sprig of thyme	1 onion
10 peppercorns	salt and vinegar

Clean and prepare the mackerel and arrange in a pie-dish, chop the onion and parsley and sprinkle over the fish. Add other ingredients with salt to taste. Pour over sufficient vinegar to cover well and bake in a moderate oven for 40 or 50 minutes. When cooked put fish carefully on a dish and strain vinegar over them. Leave until cold and serve.

EGGS WITH HADDOCK

Take one large haddock, simmer in a saucepan, thicken with flour, season to taste, place the egg on the haddock, pour the milk round and serve hot.

FISH PUDDING

½ lb of cod   1 oz of bread crumbs
2 oz suet   1 egg
½ tsp of chopped parsley seasoning
½ gill of milk (one eighth of a pint)

Bone and skin the fish, chop the suet finely, pound all ingredients well together, and when mixed put into a pudding basin, steam for an hour, serve with white sauce.

DIPPIE

Take pilchards and potatoes. Clean the fish, peel and cut up the potatoes. Then simmer them together in a pan of thin cream until they are soft.

BAKED MACKEREL

4-6 fresh mackerel	2-3 tblsp of finely
butter	chopped parsley
seasoning	flour

Clean, head and tail the fish. Mix the finely chopped parsley with 2 to 3 tablespoonsful of soft butter. Lay the fish in a well-buttered baking dish, and dust lightly with the flour. Season to taste with salt and pepper. Dot with butter, cover with well buttered paper and bake in a hot oven until the fish flakes easily with a fork.

MARINATED PILCHARDS

3 or more pilchards	bay leaves
vinegar	seasoning
cold tea	tsp brown sugar

Clean the fish, [do not split fully open], with fresh water, inside and out. Sprinkle with salt and pepper, and place a bay leaf inside each one. Put them in a baking dish or earthenware pan, and nearly cover with equal quantities of vinegar and cold tea. Add a little brown sugar and cook in a slow oven until the bones are soft. Must be eaten cold. Herring and mackerel can be cooked the same way.

FISH CAKES

1lb of cold fish	1 oz of butter
½ lb of mashed potatoes	1 egg
1 tblsp of chopped parsley	tomato sauce
bread crumbs	beef dripping for frying

Chop the fish, mix with the mashed potatoes, melt the butter in the pan, when hot, add the fish, potatoes and parsley, seasoning to taste. Put in the beaten egg, and stir over the fire until the mixture feels firm, turn out on to a plate to cool. Then shape into round, flat cakes, brush over with the egg and cover with bread crumbs. Fry in boiling fat and serve with tomato sauce.

ROAST BREAM

1 nice size bream	a little parsley
a little suet	a few bread crumbs
seasoning	

Clean and scale the bream, chop parsley and suet. Stuff bream with suet, parsley and bread crumbs. Put into a baking dish, sprinkle with suet and salt. Bake in an oven until a golden brown, dripping [basting] continually. This dish goes well with boiled potatoes.

COD'S HEAD AND SHOULDERS

1 large cod's head   seasoning
and shoulders   lemons

Cleanse the fish thoroughly, and rub a little salt over the the thick part and inside the fish 1 or 2 hours before dressing it, as this much improves the flavour. Lay it in the fish-kettle, with sufficient water to cover it. Be very particular not to pour the water on to the fish as it is liable to break, and keep it only just simmering. If the water should boil away, add a little, pouring it in at the side of the kettle, and not on to the fish. Skim very carefully, draw to the side of the fire, and let it gently simmer till done. Garnish with cut lemon and serve with oyster or caper sauce. Time 20 to 25 minutes according to size.

TO BOIL A CRAB

Have a large pan of boiling water and a handful of salt, and plunge the crab into it. Let it boil for about twenty minutes. It is better to put the crab on its feet while it is boiling.

LIMPETS

Carefully wash all the sand off the limpets, put on the fire in a pan of cold water, and boil until they slip out of their shells. Serve cold with vinegar, pepper and brown bread.

SAND EELS (LANCES)

Pinch off the head, wash and dry. Fry and serve with a squeeze of lemon.

To cure: soak in strong brine solution for 12 hours. String together with needle and twine in lots of 20 to 30. Dry in the sun. When needed, broil or soak overnight in water, and then boil.

PIES

A CORNISH PASTY

4 oz of plain flour	2 oz of fat
water to mix	4 oz of finely chopped beef
1 small potato	salt and pepper
½ small onion	
1 small piece of diced turnip (swede)	

Make pastry and roll into a ring. Take care not to roll too thinly. Spread the meat evenly over half of the pastry ring, leaving ½ an inch all round. Place the diced vegetables on top, add seasoning and either a few knobs of fat or sprinkle with water. Moisten the edges with water and fold one half over to meet the other half. Press the edges together and crimp. Brush with milk or egg and make a small hole in the top to allow steam to escape. Place on baking sheet put in top of a hot oven (200C) for 15 minutes. Reduce heat to 160C for a further 45 minutes.

TRIPE PIE

tripe	pastry
1 slice of ham or steak	4 knobs of butter
seasoning	brown gravy

Stew the tripe well before use, and leave it to jelly in its own liquid. Line the inside of a pie dish with pastry, put a slice of tender steak or ham at the bottom of the dish, and place the tripe over with the jellied gravy clinging to it. Season with pepper and salt, put pieces of butter over the tripe and pour in two or three spoonfuls of brown gravy. Cover with a good pie crust, and bake till brown. Serve piping hot.

MUGGETY PIE

intestines of a pig	2 large onions
pastry	seasoning

Take the intestines of a pig and wash them well. Cut up, and lay in the bottom of a pie-dish with plenty of sliced onions, pepper and salt. Cover with a pastry top and bake for about one hour.

LIKKY PIE

12 leeks	½ lb of green bacon
½ lb of cream	2 eggs
milk for gravy	suet crust

Take the leeks and cut them into small pieces, scald each for about ten minutes in boiling water. Cut bacon into thin slices. Put a layer of bacon in the bottom of a pie-dish, then a layer of leeks and continue until the dish is full. Season with pepper and salt. Cover with suet crust. Have ready ½ lb of cream, two well beaten eggs. When pie is cooked. take off the crust and drain off all the liquid from the pie - and substitute with cream and eggs.

CONGER PIE

4 lbs of fillet	2 tsp of salt
and skinned conger	1 pint of thin cream
1lb of boiled mashed potatoes	2 knobs of butter

Place a layer of conger in the bottom of a buttered pie dish, followed by a layer of potato, and so on - finishing with a layer of potato. Pour a pint of cream over the top and bake in a moderate oven for ½ an hour.

RABBIT PIE

1 rabbit   ½ lb of bacon or pickled pork

½ pint of stock   seasoning

short crust or puff pastry

Wash the rabbit and divide into small joints. Dice the pork. Place the ingredients in layers in a pie-dish, season each layer liberally with salt and pepper, and three quarters fill the dish with stock. Cover with paste (pastry), and bake for 1¼ to 1½ hours in a brisk oven (450F) until the pastry has risen and set. Afterwards bake more slowly until golden brown on top. Before serving add the remainder of the hot stock to the pie.

SQUAB PIE

young squabs   apples

sliced onions   fat mutton

seasoning   cooking sugar

short crust pastry

Clean squabs, and put in pie dish with remainder of ingredients. Cover with a crust and bake in a hot oven. (Squabs are young pigeons)

HERBY PIE

bacon	parsley
watercress	peppercress
leeks or shallots	spinach
2 eggs	pastry crust
stock	seasoning

Line a pie-dish with bacon. Chop small and parboil or scald parsley, watercress or peppercress, leeks or shallots, or sweet leek (small quantity), spinach.

(Some people put blackcurrant leaves, potato tops or wild orange, all mixed together.)

Beat one or two eggs. Fill the dish, put one or two layers more of streaky bacon on top and pour the beaten eggs over all. Add a little water or stock. Put on a thin pastry crust and bake according to size and thickness. Average time would be 1 ½ hours.

STAR-GAZY PIE

pilchards, mackerel or herrings
seasoning   butter
grated bread crumbs   4 slices of fat bacon
6 eggs   2 tblsp of tarragon
1 pie crust   parsley garnish
tarragon vinegar or ¼ pint of cream

Take as many pilchards, mackerel or herrings as will fill a moderate sized baking dish. Scale them and open them, and remove the bones. Lay them flat on the table, season the inside of each with salt, pepper and chopped parsley, and roll it up neatly. Butter the pie-dish and sprinkle on it a thick layer of finely grated bread crumbs. Lay in some of the fish, and fill the dish with alternate layers of fish and bread crumbs. Cover the contents with a few slices of fat bacon, and pour over all six eggs beaten up with two tablespoonful of tarragon vinegar. or if preferred a quarter of a pint of cream. Cover the dish with a good crust and bake in a well heated oven. Arrange the heads of the fish in the centre of the pastry to 'star gaze'. When the pie is baked, put a piece of parsley into the mouth of each fish and serve.

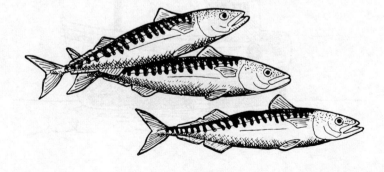

GIBLET PIE

giblets 2 pairs	1 quart water
20 peppercorns	3 blades of mace
1 large onion	bundle of sweet herbs
1 rump steak	1 pie crust

Clean two pairs of giblets well, and put all but the livers into a saucepan, with a quart of water, twenty corns of a whole pepper, three blades of mace, a bundle of sweet herbs, and a large onion. Cover them tight and stew very gently till they are tender. Have a good crust ready. Cover your dish, lay at the bottom a fine rump steak seasoned with pepper and salt, put in your giblets with the livers, and strain the liquor they stewed in; then season with salt, and pour into the pie. Put the lid on and bake for an hour and a half.

MEAT DISHES

POOR MAN'S GOOSE

½ lb of ox liver	1 onion
1 lb of potatoes	flour
½ tsp of sage	seasoning

Slice the liver, dip in flour and place the slices in a pie dish. Parboil the onion with sage, then pour over the liver with sufficient liquid to come halfway up the dish. Slice the potatoes, put over the liver to form a crust, and bake for 1 hour.

This will be found to be most appetising, and equal in taste to Goose.

BEEF AND HAM SAUSAGES

½ lb of raw beef	½ lb of smoked ham
½ lb of bread crumbs	1 tsp of salt
1 egg	½ tsp of pepper
½ teaspoonful of nutmeg	

Mix all together, add the egg. Beat up and form into a smooth roll like sausage, tie into a cloth and place in a saucepan of boiling water, leave to simmer for two hours. Take off cloth while hot, and brush over with brown bread crumbs.

CORNISH UNDER ROAST

1 lb of chuck steak	chopped onion
or streaky pork	slices of raw potato
bacon fat	stock
seasoned flour	

Cut the meat into thin strips and roll in the seasoned flour. Cover with chopped onion, and slices of raw potato brushed with bacon fat or with oil. Pour over stock, or a little cold water until almost covered. Add salt and pepper to taste, and bake in a moderate oven for 1½ hours.

PRESSED BEEF

4 lbs of brisket   a handful of salt

gravy

Cook the brisket in the oven for four hours, covered with water and a handful of salt. Take out and bone, then put into a dish with as much gravy as possible. Place a plate on top with a weight resting on the plate. Leave to stand for twelve hours, then turn out and serve cold.

SHEEPS' BRAINS

6 sheeps brains	1 pint of white stock
2 ozs of butter	1½ ozs of flour
1 tsp of finely-chopped	1 tsp of lemon-juice
parsley	½ a small onion
1 small carrot	1 bay leaf
salt and pepper	

Soak the brains in salt and water for 2 hours, then remove the skin and fibres, cover them with boiling water, and boil for 3 minutes. Replace the brains in fresh cold water and let them remain there until cold. Then put into the boiling stock, add the onion and carrot sliced, bayleaf, salt and pepper to taste, and simmer gently for 20 minutes.

Meanwhile melt the butter in a stew-pan, add the flour and cook these for 3 or 4 minutes without browning. Drain the brains, and strain the stock on to the flour and butter and stir until boiling, simmer for ten minutes - add the lemon-juice and seasoning to taste. Re-heat the brains in the sauce and, just before serving add the lemon juice.

TRIPE AND ONIONS

1 lb of tripe	½ lb of onions
1 pint of milk	salt and pepper
a little flour	potatoes

Wash the tripe. Boil for ½ an hour, strain off the water, add the milk and onions together with salt and pepper. Simmer for 1 hour. Mix the flour with a little milk and stir in. Simmer for 15 minutes more, and serve with boiled potatoes.

SEASON PUDDING

12 oz of beef	a few sprigs of
salt and pepper	parsley
½ lb of flour	4 oz of suet
gravy powder	potatoes

Cut up the beef. Put into a basin with the chopped up parsley.
Add salt and pepper, a little flour and gravy powder. Mix flour, suet and a little salt together to make a stiff dough. Roll out and put on top. Seal the edges, tie down with a cloth and boil for 2½ hours. Serve with potatoes, cabbage and peas.

PUDDINGS

QUEEN OF PUDDINGS

3 ozs of bread crumbs	1 oz of butter
2 eggs	½ pint of milk
1 oz of sugar	a little jam
a few drops of vanilla flavouring	

Boil the milk with the butter and pour over crumbs, add yolk of egg and sugar. Pour into a greased pie-dish, and bake until set. Spread the top with jam. Beat whites to a stiff froth and pile on top of the pudding. Return to oven for two or three minutes to set and slightly brown.

MARMALADE AND GOLDEN PUDDING

¼ lb of flour	¼ lb bread crumbs
¼ lb suet	¼ lb of sugar
¼ lb marmalade	1 egg
1 pint of milk	a pinch of salt.
1 teaspoonful of baking powder	

Chop suet, mix all dry ingredients together, beat egg and add milk to it, stir well into the pudding with the marmalade. Put into a greased basin, cover with a cloth and steam for two hours.

FIGGY PUDDING

2 oz of self raising flour	4 oz suet
3 figs chopped well	2 tsp allspice
4 oz breadcrumbs	8 oz of raisins
½ oz of sugar	grated rind of 1 lemon
2 beaten eggs	1 tablespoonful of sherry
	a little milk.

Mix all the dry ingredients together. Stir in the eggs and sherry and add just enough milk to make a soft dough. Place in a buttered pudding basin and cover with a greaseproof paper, allowing room for the pudding to swell. Steam for 3½ hours and serve hot.

BOILED APPLE PUDDING

½ lb of breadcrumbs	½ lb fine chopped suet
½ lb of apples	½ lb moist sugar
2 eggs	½ pint of milk
pinch of salt	good pinch of nutmeg

Pare, core and chop the apples coarsely. Mix all the dry ingredients together, add the well beaten eggs, and the milk, and mix well. Let the mixture stand for 1 hour for the bread to soak pour into a well greased basin, and steam for 2 hours.

BAKED BREAD PUDDING

8 oz of stale bread	4 oz of raisins
2 oz of finely chopped suet	2 oz of sugar
1 egg	a little milk
a good pinch of nutmeg	

Break the bread into small pieces, cover them with cold water, soak for half an hour, then strain and squeeze dry. Beat all the lumps with a fork, and stir in the sugar, suet, raisins and nutmeg. Mix well. Add the egg previously beaten, and as much milk as is necessary to make the mixture moist enough to drop readily off a spoon. Pour into a greased pie-dish and bake gently for about 1 hour. When done, turn out on to a hot dish, and drench well with sugar.

BOILED LEMON PUDDING

6 oz of bread crumbs	¼ lb of suet
2 oz of sugar	2 oz of flour
the rind and juice of 2 lemons	1 egg

Mix well and boil for 3 hours.

BIRTHDAY PUDDING

1 lb of flour	6 oz of chopped suet
3 oz of chopped mixed peel	6 oz of sultanas
6 oz of currants	grating of nutmeg
good pinch of salt	4 oz brown sugar
teacup Cornish cream	

Mix all well together and make into a stiff paste with milk. Place into scalded and floured cloth, and tie loosely, plunge into boiling water and boil for three hours. When dished up take out a piece as large as a teacup from the top. Place inside 4 ozs of coarse brown sugar, and teacup of Cornish cream. Put into the oven for two minutes and serve piping hot.

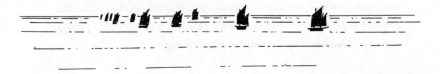

HELSTON PUDDING

2 ozs raisins	2 ozs currants
2 ozs suet	2 ozs bread crumbs
2 ozs ground rice	small piece of
2 ozs of flour	candied peel
1/2 tsp of bicarbonate of soda	1/2 tsp of mixed spice
a little salt and milk	

Clean fruit and cut peel finely. Dissolve soda in the milk, mix together all the dry ingredients and add milk. Pour all into a well greased basin, cover with greased paper and a floured pudding cloth. Stand in a saucepan of boiling water and boil for two hours.

TREACLE SPONGE PUDDING

1/4 lb of flour	2 oz of suet
1 tsp of Demerara sugar	a pinch of salt
1/2 saltspoonful of	1/2 teacupful of milk
bicarbonate of soda	1/2 teacupful of treacle

Grate the suet very finely and mix with it the flour, sugar and salt, then mix with the treacle. Get the milk just lukewarm, dissolve the bicarbonate of soda in it, and beat in the other ingredients. When well mixed put it into a well greased basin. The basin should be only three quarters full to allow for rising. Steam for 3 hours, turn out on to a dish, and pour a little golden syrup around.

CAKES

CHRISTMAS CAKE

2 lbs of flour	2 lbs of sugar
2 lbs of butter	4 lbs of currants
2 lbs of sultanas	½ lb of almonds
½ lb of citron peel	1 lb of lemon peel
1 nutmeg	¼ oz of allspice
¼ oz of cinnamon	18 eggs

Beat the butter and sugar to a soft cream, drop in the flour gradually, then the spices and the fruit. Beat the yolks of the eggs, stir into the mixture. Lastly beat the whites of the eggs, stir in very lightly; if too stiff add a little milk. If baked as one cake, bake in a moderate oven for 5 to 6 hours, or longer if it is a deep cake. If baked in smaller sizes, bake for 3 or 4 hours according to the size.

CORNISH HEAVY CAKE

1½ lbs of flour	¼ lb of cream or butter
¼ lb of beef dripping	1 tsp of salt
2 dstp of sugar	¾ lb of currants
small twist of lemon peel	

Do not put the cream and beef dripping too fine in the flour; after it is mixed with water roll it out, and then roll it up and put it aside for an hour or so. Roll it out again, and cut across with a knife. The cake will then be light and shaley. bake for 20-30 minutes according to size.

HOT CINNAMON CAKE

1½ ozs of butter - creamed	1½ ozs of sugar
1 teacup of milk	cinnamon
1 egg (white and yolk to be beaten separately)	
2 teacups of flour sifted with 2 tsp of baking powder	

Roll the dough out one inch thick, scatter sugar and cinnamon on top. Bake for 20 minutes, split - butter thickly and serve hot.

SAFFRON CAKE

2 lbs of flour	1 lb of butter
2 tsp of baking powder	¼ lb of sugar
1 lb of sultanas	1 oz of yeast
warm milk	

2 oz of mixed peel finely shredded

½ a drachm of saffron cut up very fine

and steeped in a cup of boiling water overnight

Rub fat thoroughly into the flour and sugar, and a good pinch of salt. Put yeast into a cup with a teaspoonful sugar, add a little warm milk. When the yeast rises in the cup, make a pit in the flour and pour the yeast in, together with a little more warm milk. Turn a little flour over it. When this cracks and the yeast sponges through, mix it into a soft dough by hand - using milk as required. Add the saffron whilst mixing. Then add the fruit, cover with a warm plate, and stand in a warm place until the mixture raises the plate and appears light and spongy.

Allow to rise for a short time before baking - bake for three-quarters or one hour depending on size.

GINGERBREAD NUTS

¾ lb of self raising flour	¼ lb of butter
¼ lb of brown sugar	¼ lb of syrup
½ oz of ground ginger	1 egg

Melt the butter, sugar, syrup and ginger well together, and while it is warm mix in the flour, and add the egg well beaten. Leave the mixture for one hour - or until it is cold and stiff. Flour the hands and roll the paste into small balls, place these in a greased tin and bake for about 20 minutes in a moderately quick oven. They will flatten in the oven so do not bake too hard. When cold store in a tin.

SEEDY CAKE

½ lb of flour	3 oz of butter
1 dstp caraway seeds	1 tsp of baking
3 eggs	powder
4 ozs of castor sugar	

Beat the butter and sugar to a cream, beat the yolks of the eggs well and add with flour and baking powder, whisk whites to a stiff froth, and mix lightly in, add caraway seeds, pour into a tin lined with greased paper, bake in a moderate oven for 1½ hours.

BLACK CAKE

½ lb of flour	1 lb of currants
½ lb of castor sugar	6 oz of butter
¼ lb of mixed peel	a few drops of almond
1 tsp carbonate of soda essence	1 tsp of ground rice
1 tblsp baking powder	3 eggs

Melt the butter and beat in the eggs. Burn two pieces of loaf sugar, add a little water and mix the cake with it. This has the tendency to make the cake black. Bake for 3 hours in a slow oven.

CHEESE CAKE

½ pint of good curd	4 eggs
3 spoonfuls of rich cream	1 spoonful of ratafia
½ lb of currants	½ oz of grated nutmeg
puff pastry	

Beat ½ pint of good curd with 4 eggs, the cream, ratafia and currants. add the grated nutmeg. Mix altogether and bake in patty tins with a good puff paste.

CORNISH PARKIN

10 oz fine oatmeal flour	6 oz flour
5 oz of butter	2 level tsp of
1/3 rd pint of milk	ground ginger
4 oz of black treacle	2 oz of brown sugar
1 egg	1 level tsp of salt
1 tsp of bicarbonate of soda	4 oz of golden syrup

Put the milk in a pan, add the butter, syrup and treacle. Melt slowly. Put the oatmeal in a bowl and sieve in the rest of the dry ingredients. Stir in the beaten egg and the melted ingredients. Pour into a lined tin, and bake at 150C for 1½ hours.

POTATO CAKE

1 lb of potato flour	½ lb of butter
½ lb of castor sugar	beaten to a cream
2 eggs or the whites of 4	10 drops essence of lemon

Mix the ingredients and beat thoroughly for 10 minutes; then pour into a cake-tin, and bake for 15 minutes in a rather quick oven.

PORTER CAKE

2 eggs	½ lb of butter
¾ lb of flour	1½ lbs of currants
½ tsp of mixed spice	½ pint of stout (warmed)
heaped tsp of bicarbonate of soda	

Melt the butter but don't allow to boil. Add sugar, add the stout, and the well beaten eggs. Add the flour and sugar together. Add all the ingredients and mix well for ten minutes. Place in two or three small tins and bake in a moderate oven for 2 to 2½ hours.

FARMHOUSE CIDER CAKE

8oz of flour	1 tsp bicarbonate of soda
2 eggs	½ tsp of grated
4 oz of sugar	nutmeg
4 oz butter	1 teacup of still cider

Beat the butter and sugar to a cream, add the eggs, then halve the flour into which has been sieved the nutmeg and bicarbonate of soda. Beat the cider to a froth, then pour over the mixture. Stir in the remainder of the flour and mix well. Bake in a greased cake tin in a moderate oven for 45 minutes.

SODA CAKE

8 oz flour	pinch of salt
5 oz of butter	5 oz sugar
6 oz currants	1 egg
½ tsp bicarbonate of soda	½ tsp of cream of tartar
½ tsp grated nutmeg	sour milk to mix

Sieve the dry ingredients, rub in the fat, add sugar and fruit. Mix with beaten egg and sour milk to a dropping consistency. Put into a 6 inch cake tin and bake in a moderate oven for about an hour. In place of sour milk 1 small teaspoonful of lemon-juice or a few drops of vinegar, can be added to ½ pint of fresh milk which is then left to stand overnight.

VINEGAR CAKE

1 lb flour	½ lb of butter or dripping
¼ lb of raisins	½ lb of currants
½ lb of sugar	½ pint of milk
3 tblsp of vinegar	1 tsp of bicarb.

Sieve the flour, rub in the fat, and add the fruit and sugar. Put the milk into a large jug, and add the vinegar. Mix the bicarbonate of soda with a little milk and pour into the mixed milk and vinegar. It will froth up, and while still frothing stir into the other ingredients. Pour into a well-greased tin, and bake in a moderate oven for 1 hour.

SCONES AND QUICK BREADS

RASPBERRY BUNS

2 oz of butter	2 oz of sugar
½ lb of flour	1 egg
¼ pint of milk	½ tsp of baking
raspberry jam	powder

Rub the butter into the flour, add the sugar and the baking powder, mix stiffly with the beaten egg and milk. Divide into buns and and place on a greased baking sheet, making a hole in the centre of each bun. Drop in a little jam and cover up again. Bake in a moderate oven for 15 to 20 minutes.

CORNISH SANDWICHES

2 spoonfuls of damson, whortleberry,
or blackberry jam
2 spoonfuls of clotted cream
8 small scones, fresh but cold

Rub the jam through a sieve, split the scones and remove part of the soft inside. Spread a little jam on each half of the scone, and teaspoonful of thick cream on the lower half of each, press the scones together. Prepare shortly before they are to be eaten.

CORNISH SPLITS

1 lb of flour	1 oz of butter
1/2 oz of yeast	1/2 oz of castor sugar
1/2 pint of tepid milk	1/2 tsp salt

Cream the yeast and the milk together until they are liquid, sieve the flour and a quarter teaspoonful of salt into a basin. Melt the butter gently, add it and the milk to the flour, and mix it all into a smooth dough. Put the basin into a warm place and let the dough rise for of an hour. Shape into small round cakes and place in a floured baking tin. Bake in a quick oven for 15 to 20 minutes. Split and butter them. Serve very hot, or leave until cold. Then split and butter them and eat with cream, jam or treacle. Splits eaten with cream and treacle are known as 'Thunder and lightning.'

NUT BREAD

4 cups of flour	2 cups of milk
½ lb of sugar	1 tsp of salt
4 tsp of baking powder	1 egg
1 walnut crushed small	

Mix the dry ingredients together, add the egg to the milk and then stir all together. Set to stand for 20 minutes and then bake in a moderate oven for one hour.

CORNISH FAIRINGS

4 oz of flour	1 tsp of baking powder
2 oz of butter	
1 tsp of bicarbonate of soda	a pinch of salt
½ tsp of mixed spice	2 oz of castor sugar
1 tsp of ground ginger	3 tblsp of golden syrup

Mix the bicarbonate of soda and the spices, sieve with the flour and add the sugar, mix together thoroughly. Rub in the butter. Warm the syrup slightly, pour it into a warm spoon and then stir into the mixture to make a stiff paste. Roll the final mix into strips about an inch thick, and cut off into pieces an inch long. Place on a greased baking tray and bake in a hot oven.

POTATO SCONES

6 oz of flour   3 oz of mashed potato

2 tsp of baking powder   2 oz of butter

a little milk.

Sieve the flour and baking powder, rub in the fat, add the mashed potato and enough milk to work into a stiff dough. Turn out on to a well floured board, roll out to about inch thick, cut with a pastry cutter and bake on a greased baking sheet for 12-15 minutes in a hot oven.

CORNISH HOT CAKES

8 oz of freshly boiled potatoes   4 oz of plain flour

2 oz of chopped suet   2 oz of sultanas

1 egg   1 tsp of baking powder

Sieve the potato while hot, sieve the flour with the baking powder, add to the mashed potato and the suet. Add the fruit, mix well and bind to a firm dough with the beaten egg. Roll out on to a floured board to about 1" thickness. Place in a greased tin, and score deeply into squares. Bake for about 1 hour until golden brown in a hot oven.

ALMOND FINGERS

2 oz of butter	2 oz of sugar
5 oz of flour	a pinch of salt
½ tsp of almond essence	

Cream the butter and the sugar, work in the flour to form a soft dough. Add the almond essence, and knead it. Roll-out a quarter of an inch thick, and cut into three inch long fingers. Bake in a moderate oven until pale brown.

EASTER BISCUITS

8 oz of plain flour	3 oz of sultanas
4 oz of castor sugar	1 egg
grated rind of ½ lemon	4 oz of unsalted butter

Cream the butter and the sugar, add the lemon rind. Gradually beat in the egg and the flour, then work in the sultanas to produce a stiff dough. Roll out the paste and cut into biscuit shapes with a cutter. Bake at 170C for 15 minutes.

GINGER BISCUITS

½ lb of flour	¼ lb of butter
1 cup of syrup	1 tsp baking powder
1 tsp mixed spice	1 tsp bicarbonate
1 oz ground ginger	of soda

Warm the syrup and beat the bicarbonate of soda into it. Mix all ingredients together and roll into small balls the size of a walnut. Grease the sheet and bake for 15 minutes.

BEVERAGES

CORNISH PUNCH

1 bottle of Jamaica Rum	½ bottle of Cognac
1 tumbler of lemon juice	a little of the rind
2-4 lbs of sugar to taste	a little Benedictine

Put in the sugar, pour in the lemon juice and rind. Put in the brandy and the rum. The whole put into a one gallon jug, and fill up with boiling water poured from a height.

MAHOGANY

Mix together one cup of treacle with two cups of gin - beat well together. Traditionally this drink was served with pilchards.

SHENAGRUM

Take 2 lumps of sugar, 1 wineglass of rum, 2 slices of lemon with rind. Fill the glass with boiled beer.

HERBY BEER

A large handful of young stinging nettles
Yarrow and wild sage   1½ lbs of sugar
2 oz of yeast   2 gallons of water

Take two gallons of water, add herbs, boil all together and then add 1½ lbs of sugar. When nearly cold add 2 ozs of yeast, and let it all stand till next day. Then strain through muslin, bottle and cork. Tie the corks down firmly. It must not be drunk until at least three days old.

SAMPSON

1 quart of strong cider   2 eggs
1 tblsp of sugar

Heat the cider in a large saucepan. Beat up the eggs with the tablespoonful of sugar in a large jug. When the cider is hot pour a portion on to the beaten eggs and then back to the pan again, and so on until the whole is a frothy mixture.

EGGIOT

1 egg   1 tsp sugar
½ pint of milk

Beat up the egg in a tumbler, add 1 teaspoonful of sugar, heat half-pint of milk and before it reaches boiling point pour on the beaten egg, stirring briskly.

ALE PUNCH

1 quart of old ale   1 pint boiling water
¼ pint of rum   ¼ pint of whisky
¼ pint of gin   1 lemon thinly sliced
sugar to taste   pinch ground cinnamon
pinch of ground cloves

Put all the ingredients in a large stew-pan, and bring nearly to boiling point. Strain into a punch bowl, add a few lemon slices and serve.

OVEN TEMPERATURES

	Fahrenheit	Gas Mark	Celsius
Slow	300	2	140
	325	3	160
Moderate	350	4	180
	375	5	190
	400	6	200
Hot	425	7	210
	450	8	230
	500	9	260

Granny of course knew that a piece of white paper in a very hot oven turned golden brown in around a minute.

An oven rated hot turned the paper golden brown in about three minutes.

A moderate oven took about five minutes, and a slow oven seven to eight minutes.

ACKNOWLEDGMENTS

Four books have been of particular interest to me in compiling this small collection of recipes. A paperback book produced by the Cornwall Federation of Women's Institutes ran through no less than thirteen editions between April 1929 and August 1936 - 'Cornish Recipes, Ancient and Modern.' It has become almost the accepted reference work for anyone writing about Cornish cuisine.

Likewise, the Centenary Wesleyan Recipe Book which sold for one shilling in 1922, filled in for me the background to many of the recipes I was offered.

A.K.Hamilton Jenkin published three titles in the early 1930's - and they have become standard books on the history and lore of Cornwall. They are Cornish Seafarers, Cornwall and the Cornish, and Cornish Homes and Customs.

Last, but not least. My thanks are due to Jessie Gross, Elsie and Gina Hodge, Freddie May, Maisie Rendle, Gwen and Arthur Rowse, and Jack Spurr.

INDEX

Rabbit Pie	18
Raspberry Buns	40
Roast Bream	12
Saffron Cake	33
Sampson	47
Sand Eels	13
Season Pudding	25
Seedy Cake	34
Sheeps Brains	24
Shenagrum	46
Soda Cake	38
Squab Pie	18
Star-Gazy Pie	20
Treacle Sponge Pudding	30
Tripe and Onions	25
Tripe Pie	16
Vinegar Cake	39